Conserving Resources

Printed in México

ISBN-13: 978-0-15-362028-7

ISBN-10: 0-15-362028-5

7 8 9 10 0908 16 15 14 13 12 11
4500330476

Harcourt
SCHOOL PUBLISHERS

Visit *The Learning Site!*
www.harcourtschool.com

What Are Some Types of Resources?

VOCABULARY

resource
renewable
 resources
reusable
 resources
nonrenewable
 resources

A **resource** is something found in nature that is used by living things. Trees are a resource.

Renewable resources are resources that can be replaced within a person's lifetime. Animals are renewable resources.

Reusable resources are resources that can be used again and again. Water is a reusable resource.

Nonrenewable resources are resources that cannot be replaced in a short period of time. When they are used up, there will be no more. Oil is a nonrenewable resource.

Resources

   A **resource** is something found in nature that is used by living things. Animals are resources. People use them for food and clothing. Plants are also resources. They are used for food and to make things, such as paper and clothes.

Grass is a resource for cows.
Cows are a resource for people. ▼

4

Water is an important resource. So are air, rocks, metals, oil, and salt.

Resources are found in many places. Some resources are above ground. Others are below ground.

Oil is pumped from underground. It is used to make gasoline. ▶

Focus Skill **Tell why plants and animals are resources.**

People grow plants for food. ▼

Renewable Resources

Some resources can be replaced. Others cannot. **Renewable resources** can be replaced during a person's lifetime.

Plants and animals are renewable resources. Some kinds of energy are renewable resources, too. Energy from the sun is a renewable resource.

 Name three renewable resources.

Trees are renewable resources.

Reusable Resources

Reusable resources can be used again and again. Air and water are two reusable resources.

After water is used, it is polluted. A water treatment plant can clean water. Then it can be used again.

Cars and factories can pollute the air. Plants, wind, and rain help clean the air. Then it is safe to breathe again.

 What are some kinds of reusable resources?

Water is a reusable resource.

Nonrenewable Resources

Nonrenewable resources are resources that cannot be replaced in a human lifetime. When they are used up, there will be no more.

Gasoline is a nonrenewable resource. One day the oil used to make gas will all be gone. Coal, soil, and metals are also nonrenewable resources.

 What are some nonrenewable resources?

▼ Metal is often dug
out of the ground.

▲ Coal takes thousands of years to form.
People dig it out of the ground.

Review

Focus Skill

Complete this main idea statement.

1. Living things use many kinds of _____ in order to live.

Complete these detail statements.

2. _____ resources can be replaced.

3. Water and air are _____ resources that can be used again and again.

4. A _____ resource, such as metal, cannot be replaced.

What Are Some Types of Soil?

VOCABULARY

humus
sand
silt
clay
loam

Humus is the part of soil made up of bits of dead plants and animals.

Sand is grains of rock that you can see with your eyes. Sand covers many beaches.

Silt is grains of rock that are too small to see with your eyes.

Clay is very, very tiny grains of rock.

Loam is soil that is a mixture of humus, sand, silt, and clay. Loam is used to grow fruits and vegetables.

READING FOCUS SKILL
COMPARE AND CONTRAST

When you compare and contrast, you tell how things are alike and different.

Look for ways to compare and contrast types of soil.

Layers of Soil

Soil is an important resource. Plants need soil to grow. Many animals live in soil.

Soil is a mixture. It is made up of water, air, tiny rocks, and humus. **Humus** is made up of bits of dead plants and animals.

Plants grow in soil. ▼

Soil forms in layers. Soil near the top has a lot of humus. Deeper down, soil has less humus and more rocks.

 Tell how soil near the surface is different from soil deeper down.

Layers of Soil

Soil on top has a lot of humus.

Soil below has less humus, but more small pieces of rock.

Deep below soil is solid rock.

Different Types of Soil

There are many kinds of soil. Soils have different colors. Some soils hold more water than others. Soils also have different sizes of rocks in them. The rock sizes make the soil feel different.

Sandy soil ▼

Clay soil has tiny grains of rock.

There are three main types of soil. The main difference among them is the size of rocks in them.

Sand is soil with grains of rock that you can see with your eyes. **Silt** is soil with grains of rock you can barely see with your eyes. **Clay** is soil with tiny mineral grains too small to see.

Focus Skill **Tell how sand, silt, and clay soils are alike and different.**

The Importance of Soil

Soil is important to many living things. Plants grow in soil. Many animals make their homes in soil.

Farmers use soil to grow crops. ▼

Soil is also important to people. We use soil to make bricks and pottery. We also use soil to grow many foods. Loam is the best soil to grow crops. **Loam** is a mixture of humus, clay, silt, and sand.

 Tell different ways people use soil.

▲ Most crops are grown in loam.

Review

Complete these compare and contrast statements.

1. Soil of all kinds is an important _____.

2. The top layer of soil usually has more _____ than the other layers.

3. The grains of rock in _____ are larger than those in silt.

4. _____ is soil that has the smallest grains of rock.

How Do People Use and Impact the Environment?

Pollution is any harmful material in the environment. Smoke can cause air pollution.

READING FOCUS SKILL

CAUSE AND EFFECT

A **cause** is what makes something happen. An **effect** is what happens.

Look for some **effects** people have on the environment.

Uses of the Land

People use land in different ways. People build on land. They use resources from land, such as wood, rock, and metal, to make buildings.

People also use land to grow plants. Plants are used for food and to make medicine and cloth.

Many people live and work on land. ▼

20

Trees help
hold soil in place. ▶

When people use land, they change it. Sometimes they change it in good ways. For example, planting trees can help hold soil in place.

Other times, people change land in bad ways. Mining can destroy land. It can harm plants and animals that live there.

 Tell how people cause changes to land.

Mining for metals can harm land. ▼

Land Pollution

People also change land in bad ways when they make pollution. **Pollution** is any harmful material in the environment.

▼ Land pollution

Many things can cause pollution. Solid wastes, gases, and noise can cause pollution.

One kind of pollution is land pollution. People throwing trash in the wrong places causes land pollution.

Land pollution can harm plants, animals, and people. It can also make water dirty.

 **Tell what causes land pollution.**

Some trash takes years to break down.

Air Pollution

Pollution can also harm air. Smoke from cars and factories causes most air pollution.

Air pollution can make it hard for people to breathe. It can also change the weather. Smoke traps heat from sunlight. This makes Earth warmer.

 What causes air pollution?

◀ Polluted air

Clean air ▶

Water Pollution

Pollution can harm water, too. Trash and oil dumped in water can cause water pollution.

Polluted water is not safe to drink. It can make animals sick. Some water pollution can be cleaned up. Water treatment plants can make some polluted water clean again.

 Tell what can happen when water is polluted.

Oil spills cause water pollution. ▶

Review

 Complete these cause and effect statements.

1. When people use land, they _____ it in some way.

2. Throwing trash in the wrong place can cause _____ pollution.

3. Air pollution can make it hard for people to _____ .

4. When water is polluted, it is unsafe to _____.

How Can Resources Be Used Wisely?

Conservation is saving resources by using them wisely. Writing on both sides of paper saves trees.

Reduce means to use less of a resource. Turning off a light when you are not using it reduces the use of electiricity.

Reuse means to use a resource again and again. Bags can be reused in many ways.

Recycle means to make new things from old things. Plastic bottles and old tires can be recycled to make a playground.

READING FOCUS SKILL
MAIN IDEA AND DETAILS

A **main idea** is what the text is mostly about. **Details** tell more about the main idea.

Look for **details** about how to save resources.

Protecting Resources

People use many resources. Some resources cannot be replaced when they are used up. So it is important to protect them. Conservation is one way to do this. **Conservation** is saving resources by using them wisely.

 Tell why it is important to protect resources.

Conservation protects resources, such as water and animals. ▼

◀ Turning off lights reduces the use of electricity.

Reduce

One way to save resources is to use less of them, or reduce how much you use. To **reduce** resources means to use less of things.

There are many ways to reduce. You can take a shower instead of a bath. This saves water. You can ride a bike instead of using a car. This saves gas. Reducing now means there will be more resources for the future.

(Focus Skill) **Tell how to reduce the amount of resources used.**

Riding bikes reduces the use of gasoline. ▶

29

Reuse

Another way to save resources is to reuse them. **Reuse** means to use a resource again and again. When you reuse things, you need fewer new things made from resources. Reusing saves money, too.

 Tell why it is important to reuse resources.

▼ Reusing bags to make gift wrap saves trees.

Recycle

Recycling also saves resources. **Recycle** means to break something down and use it to make something new. You can recycle paper, glass, metal, and plastic. Paper is recycled to make cards, paper towels, and newspaper. Plastic can be recycled to make park benches.

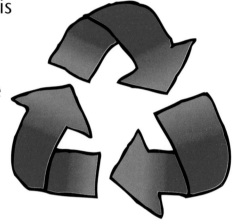

▲ Recycling symbol

 What materials can be recycled?

Review

 Complete this main idea statement.

1. _____ helps protect Earth's resources.

Complete these detail statements.

2. Riding bikes helps _____ the use of gasoline.

3. When you _____ a resource, you use it again and again.

4. You can make something new when you _____ paper, glass, or plastic.

GLOSSARY

clay (KLAY) soil with very, very tiny grains of rock (15)

conservation (kahn•ser•VAY•shuhn) saving resources by using them wisely (28)

humus (HYOO•muhs) the part of soil made up of broken-down parts of dead plants and animals (12)

loam (LOHM) soil that is a mixture of humus, sand, silt, and clay (17)

nonrenewable resource (nahn•rih•NOO•uh•buhl REE•sawrs) a resource that cannot be replaced in a human lifetime (8)

pollution (puh•LOO•shuhn) any harmful material in the environment (22)

recycle (ree•SY•kuhl) to reuse a resource by breaking it down and making a new product (31)

reduce (ree•DOOS) to use less of a resource (29)

renewable resource (rih•NOO•uh•buhl REE•sawrs) a resource that can be replaced quickly (6)

resource (REE•sawrs) a material that is found in nature and that is used by living things (4)

reusable resource (ree•YOOZ•uh•buhl REE•sawrs) a resource that can be used again and again (7)

reuse (ree•YOOZ) to use a resource again and again (30)

sand (SAND) soil with grains of rock that you can see with your eyes (15)

silt (SILT) soil with grains of rock that are too small to see with your eyes (15)

Think About the Reading

1. Describe three types of resources. Give examples of each one.
2. Explain why conserving resources is important. Then describe three ways that people can save resources.

Hands-On Activity

Collect soil samples from three different places.

1. Use a hand lens to observe the samples.
2. Label each sample and describe what it is like.

School-Home Connection

Take a walk with a family member to observe how land is used in your community. Look for evidence of land, air, and water pollution. Talk about ways to reduce trash and conserve resources in your home and community.

GRADE 3
Book 8
WORD COUNT
955
GENRE
Expository Nonfiction
LEVEL
See TG or go Online

GO online Harcourt Leveled
Readers Online Database
www.eharcourtschool.com

ISBN-13: 978-0-15-362028-7
ISBN-10: 0-15-362028-5

90000 >

9 780153 620287

Harcourt
SCHOOL PUBLISHERS